Big Dogs, Little Dogs

A Visual Guide to the World's Dogs

FIREFLY BOOKS

Jim Medway

Contents

Working Dogs

Working dogs were originally bred for jobs other than hunting and herding. These jobs might include pulling carts or guarding farm animals. 4

Hound Dogs

These dogs were the first hunting dogs. They can use either sight — their eyes — or scent — their noses — or both, to track and chase their prey. Some of the biggest hounds once hunted deer, wolves, and even lions. 6

Sporting Dogs

Sporting dogs were bred to help hunters find and bring back birds that had been shot. Different breeds can point — show the hunter where a bird is by standing still and staring — retrieve, or flush — drive birds out of their hiding places. 8

Herding Dogs

Herding dogs were first bred to herd animals — cattle and sheep. They are very good at responding to commands and whistles. 10

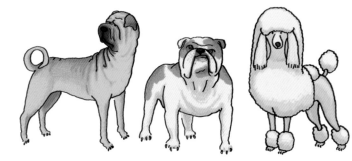

Non-sporting Dogs

These are sturdy dogs with different appearances and personalities. 12

Terrier Dogs

All terriers were originally bred to hunt rats, rabbits, and foxes both above and below ground (in tunnels). Some breeds were even trained to hunt otters and badgers. They are all small and very active. 14

Toy Dogs

These are the smallest dog breeds. Some of these were bred simply to sit on their owner's lap to warm them, and are known as lap dogs. 16

European Dogs

These dogs are all originally from Europe. They are some of the rarer breeds and include terriers, herding dogs, and sporting dogs. 18

World Dogs

These are examples of rare dogs from all over the world, including the United States, Thailand, Russia, Peru, and Japan. 20

Mixed-breed Dogs

Mixed-breed dogs are a combination of two types of popular breeds. 22

Puppies

Some puppies look very different from the adult dogs they turn into. For example, the Dalmatian is born without any spots, the Shar-pei has no rolls when it is born, and the Kerry Blue Terrier is born black. 24

Dog Breed Index

Fascinating facts about every dog breed included in the book. 26

Working Dogs

Akita

Standard Schnauzer

Mastiff

Siberian Husky

Cane Corso

Greater Swiss Mountain Dog

Boxer

Tibetan Mastiff

Boerboel

German Pinscher

Leonberger

Samoyed

Bullmastiff

Newfoundland

Giant Schnauzer

Anatolian Shepherd Dog

Komondor

Chinook

Alaskan Malamute

Great Pyrenees

St. Bernard

Kuvasz

Great Dane

Bernese Mountain Dog

Portuguese Water Dog

Dogue de Bordeaux

Doberman Pinscher

Black Russian Terrier

Neapolitan Mastiff

Rottweiler

Hound Dogs

Plott

Otterhound

Afghan Hound

American Foxhound

Greyhound

Harrier

Basset Hound

Bluetick Coonhound

Bloodhound

English Foxhound

Portuguese Podengo Pequeno

Dachshund

Scottish Deerhound

Treeing Walker Coonhound

Sloughi

American English Coonhound

Basenji

Irish Wolfhound

Ibizan Hound

Beagle

Cirneco dell'Etna

Petit Basset Griffon Vendéen

Pharaoh Hound

Black and Tan Coonhound

Whippet

Redbone Coonhound

Borzoi

Saluki

Rhodesian Ridgeback

Norwegian Elkhound

Sporting Dogs

Field Spaniel

Clumber Spaniel

English Springer Spaniel

Flat-coated Retriever

Golden Retriever

Chesapeake Bay Retriever

English Cocker Spaniel

Curly-coated Retriever

Irish Red and White Setter

Gordon Setter

Vizsla

English Setter

Spinone Italiano

German Wirehaired Pointer

Wirehaired Vizsla

Irish Setter

Brittany

Labrador Retriever

Boykin Spaniel

Nova Scotia Duck Tolling Retriever

Weimaraner

Sussex Spaniel

Lagotto Romagnolo

American Water Spaniel

Wirehaired Pointing Griffon

Cocker Spaniel

German Shorthaired Pointer

Irish Water Spaniel

Welsh Springer Spaniel

Pointer

Herding Dogs

Pyrenean Shepherd

Australian Shepherd

Australian Cattle Dog

Belgian Tervuren

Belgian Sheepdog

Bearded Collie

Belgian Malinois

Briard

Beauceron

Berger Picard

Bouvier des Flandres

Canaan Dog

Miniature American Shepherd

Border Collie

Bergamasco

Icelandic
Sheepdog

Spanish
Water Dog

Swedish
Vallhund

Puli

Finnish
Lapphund

Pembroke
Welsh Corgi

Shetland
Sheepdog

Norwegian
Buhund

Old
English
Sheepdog

Entlebucher
Mountain Dog

Collie

German
Shepherd
Dog

Polish
Lowland
Sheepdog

Cardigan
Welsh Corgi

Non-sporting Dogs

Chow Chow

Tibetan Spaniel

Dalmatian

Shiba Inu

Bulldog

Poodle

Tibetan Terrier

Lhasa Apso

Schipperke

Boston Terrier

12

French Bulldog

Xoloitzcuintli

Bichon Frise

Löwchen

Keeshond

Finnish Spitz

Chinese Shar-pei

Coton de Tulear

Norwegian Lundehund

American Eskimo Dog

Terrier Dogs

Cesky Terrier

Irish Terrier

American Staffordshire Terrier

Airedale Terrier

Kerry Blue Terrier

Border Terrier

Sealyham Terrier

Manchester Terrier

Parson Russell Terrier

Norwich Terrier

Wire Fox Terrier

Rat Terrier

Bull Terrier

Bedlington Terrier

Dandie Dinmont Terrier

American Hairless Terrier

Miniature Schnauzer

Glen of Imaal Terrier

Russell Terrier

Scottish Terrier

Australian Terrier

Lakeland Terrier

Skye Terrier

Norfolk Terrier

Cairn Terrier

Miniature Bull Terrier

Staffordshire Bull Terrier

West Highland White Terrier

Welsh Terrier

Smooth Fox Terrier

Soft Coated Wheaten Terrier

Toy Dogs

Cavalier King Charles Spaniel

Toy Poodle

Japanese Chin

Miniature Pinscher

Pug

Pomeranian

Silky Terrier

Papillon

Affenpinscher

Toy Manchester Terrier

Brussels
Griffon

Italian
Greyhound

Toy Fox
Terrier

Yorkshire
Terrier

Chinese
Crested

Shih Tzu

Maltese

English Toy
Spaniel

Pekingese

Havanese

Chihuahua

European Dogs

Estrela Mountain Dog

Kooikerhondje

Drever

Lancashire Heeler

Barbet

Bourbonnais Pointer

Shorthaired Italian Hound

Hovawart

Hamilton Hound

Cesky Fousek

Jack Russell Terrier

Stabyhoun

German Spitz

Basset Fauve de Bretagne

Dutch Partridge Dog

Jagdterrier

Bolognese

Grand Basset
Griffon Vendéen

Karelian Bear
Dog

Italian Pointer

Pumi

Slovakian
Hound

French
Spaniel

Pyrenean
Mastiff

Large
Münsterländer

Basset Bleu
de Gascogne

Transylvanian
Hound

Portuguese
Pointer

Mudi

Bavarian
Mountain
Hound

Grand Bleu de
Gascogne

Norrbottenspets

World Dogs

Greenland Dog

Kishu Ken

Thai Ridgeback

Shikoku

American Bulldog

Black Mouth Cur

Caucasian Shepherd Dog

Australian Kelpie

Canadian Eskimo Dog

Russian Toy

American Leopard Hound

Jindo

Kai Ken

Treeing Tennessee Brindle

Peruvian Hairless Dog

Azawakh

Mountain Cur

Dogo Argentino

Mixed-breed Dogs

Sprocker

Chorkie

Dobernauzer

Yorkipoo

Cockapoo

Cavachon

Boweimar

Westiepoo

Goldendoodle

Jack Russell
Cattle Dog

Longdog

Chow Pei

Jug

Beagleman

Gerberian Shepsky

Peekapoo

Huskamute

Bug

Labradoodle

Horgi

Schnoodle

Chowman Shepherd

Puggle

Bassetmatian

Gollie

Boglen Terrier

Dorgi

Puppies

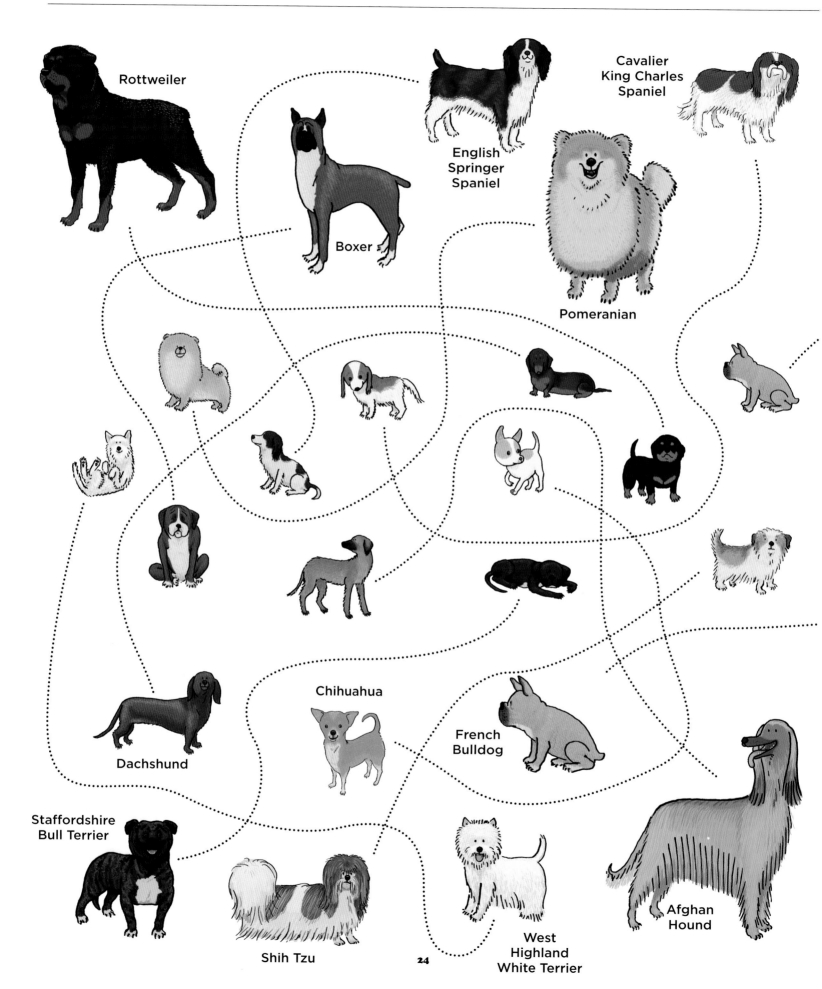

Rottweiler

English Springer Spaniel

Cavalier King Charles Spaniel

Boxer

Pomeranian

Chihuahua

French Bulldog

Dachshund

Staffordshire Bull Terrier

Shih Tzu

West Highland White Terrier

Afghan Hound

English Cocker
Spaniel

Poodle

English
Setter

Beagle

Old English
Sheepdog

Pug

Border
Terrier

Miniature
Schnauzer

German
Spitz

St.
Bernard

Bulldog

Great
Dane

Akita

Dog Breeds

Affenpinscher
This German breed's name means "Monkey Terrier." It is a sturdy little dog with a monkey-like face. 16

Afghan Hound
The Afghan is a sight hound, which means it uses its eyes to find prey. It was bred in Afghanistan thousands of years ago. 6, 24

Airedale Terrier
Known as the King of Terriers, the Airedale comes from the English county of Yorkshire. 14

Akita
The Akita became popular in the United States after World War II when American soldiers brought them home from Japan. 4, 25

Alaskan Malamute
This powerful and athletic dog was used to pull sleds in the Arctic. 5

American Bulldog
It is descended from the English Bulldog, but the American breed has longer legs. 20

American English Coonhound
Popular in the Southern United States, this Coonhound is a descendant of English Foxhounds that were brought to America in the 17th and 18th centuries. 7

American Eskimo Dog
Known as Eskies, these dogs actually have nothing to do with Eskimos, nor do they come from America. In fact they are descended from German Spitz breeds. 13

American Foxhound
The American Foxhound is a pack animal so likes the company of other dogs. 6

American Hairless Terrier
Similar to a Rat Terrier but with no hair, Hairless Terriers need protection from the sun because of their baldness. 15

American Leopard Hound
This big dog's coat is spotted like a leopard's coat. The breed is also known as the Catahoula Cur. 21

American Staffordshire Terrier
Descended from the Staffordshire Bull Terrier, which was brought from the UK in the 19th century, the American Staffordshire Terrier was bred as a heavier dog with a larger head. 14

American Water Spaniel
This waterfowl hunting dog's thick coat helps it to cope with cold water and winter temperatures. 9

Anatolian Shepherd Dog
Shepherds in remote areas in Turkey once used these large and independent dogs to protect sheep. 5

Australian Cattle Dog
This Australian dog has markings found in no other dog in the world: a blue coat with black patches around the eyes. 10

Australian Kelpie
Kelpies come in many different colors, including black, black and tan, red, blue, fawn, cream, white, and golden. 20

Australian Shepherd
Despite its name this breed does not come from Australia, but from the United States. 10

Australian Terrier
This breed is descended from Terriers brought to Australia in the early 19th century. 15

Azawakh
These noble-looking African dogs were bred to hunt in the hot deserts of the Sahara. 21

Barbet
A rare breed of French water dog, the Barbet has a thick, wooly coat. 18

Basenji
Basenjis do not bark, but instead make a yodel-like sound. They are also unusual because they do not smell. 7

Basset Bleu de Gascogne
A French hunting hound, the Blue Gascony Basset, as it is also known, was first bred in the Middle Ages. 19

Basset Fauve de Bretagne
Originally from Brittany in France, this short-legged hunting dog is similar to the Basset Hound. 18

Basset Hound
Like Bloodhounds, Basset Hounds have a powerful sense of smell. Having short legs, they can keep their noses close to the ground for sniffing while they walk or run along. 6

Bassetmatian
A cross between a Basset Hound and a Dalmatian. 23

Bavarian Mountain Hound
This big hunting dog was bred to track game in Bavaria, Germany. 19

Beagle
A scent hound, the Beagle hunts in packs, normally with hunters who are on foot rather than on horseback. Former US President Lyndon Johnson had two Beagles: one called Him and one called Her. 7, 25

Beagleman
A cross between a Beagle and a German Shepherd Dog. 22

Bearded Collie
Bearded Collies originally came from Scotland, where they were used to herd sheep. 10

Beauceron
Also known as the French Shorthaired Shepherd, this herding dog is related to the Briard. 10

Bedlington Terrier
This dog is named for the town of Bedlington in the northeast of England. It was bred to catch vermin in coal mines. 14

Belgian Malinois
An excellent dog to train, the Malinois is used by the US Secret Service. 10

Belgian Sheepdog
Also known as the Groenendael, this black sheepdog was used in World War I to deliver messages and pull carriages. 10

Belgian Tervuren
The name of this long-haired sheepdog comes from the village of Tervuren in Belgium. 10

Bergamasco
The Bergamasco has a thick coat of long, matted hair. 10

Berger Picard
A rare breed of French sheepdog, it may once have been used for smuggling goods over the French–Belgian border. 10

Bernese Mountain Dog
This big dog originally worked on Swiss farms. It thrives in a very cold climate. 5

Bichon Frise
Bichon means small long-haired dog in old French. The dogs enjoy swimming and retrieving, and are believed to have been popular with sailors. 13

Black and Tan Coonhound
Bred to trail raccoons, these black hounds are known for their calm nature. 7

Black Mouth Cur
A cattle and hunting dog, the Black Mouth Cur was bred in the southeastern part of the United States. 20

Black Russian Terrier
Developed by the Soviet military, the Black Russian is not actually a Terrier, but a large working dog bred to be used by the army. 5

Bloodhound
The Bloodhound is still used to track and find people, particularly in the United States. 6

Bluetick Coonhound
A breed from the Southern United States, Blueticks chase their prey up a tree and then bay to tell the hunter where they are. 6

Boerboel
Known as the South African Mastiff, it was created to protect farms in Africa. 4

Boglen Terrier
A cross between a Beagle and a Boston Terrier. 23

Bolognese
Named for the city of Bologna in Italy where it is thought to have come from, it is similar to the Maltese. 19

Border Collie
Collie means sheepdog in Scottish English. This is one of the most intelligent dog breeds. 10

Border Terrier
Originally used to flush out foxes, the Border Terrier can keep up with horses during a hunt. 14, 25

Barbet

Borzoi
Also known at Russian Wolfhounds, Borzoi were originally used for hunting wolves. 7

Boston Terrier
The Boston Terrier was created in Boston, Massachusetts, in the 19th century. It is believed to have been a British Bulldog and English Terrier cross. 12

Bourbonnais Pointer
Known as the short-tailed pointer, the Bourbonnais is born sometimes with a short tail, and sometimes with no tail at all. 18

Bouvier des Flandres
This compact sheepdog from Flanders has thick eyebrows and a beard. 10

Boweimar
A cross between a Boxer and a Weimaraner. 22

Boxer
The breed gets its name from its habit of standing up and "boxing" with its front paws. 4, 24

Boykin Spaniel
The State dog of California, the Boykin Spaniel was bred to work in the warm climate of the southeast of the United States. 9

Briard
The Emperor Charlemagne, Napoleon Bonaparte, and former US President Thomas Jefferson are all believed to have owned Briards. 10

Brittany
Originally from Brittany, France, this gundog can both point and retrieve for the hunter. 9

Brussels Griffon
Originally from Belgium, this small Terrier-like dog was bred to hunt mice and rats. 17

Bug
A cross between a Boston Terrier and a Pug. 23

Bull Terrier
The Bull Terrier is the only dog to have triangle-shaped eyes. It is also known for having a flat, egg-shaped head. 14

Bulldog
This breed comes from the British Isles and has a reputation for being very stubborn. 12, 25

Bullmastiff
Although it does not bark much, the Bullmastiff was originally used to guard large country estates against poachers. 4

Cairn Terrier
One of the oldest of all Terrier breeds, the Cairn Terrier comes from the Scottish Highlands. 15

Canaan Dog
The national dog of Israel, this sheepdog comes from the Middle East. The breed may

Border Collie

be over two thousand years old. 10

Canadian Eskimo Dog
Now very rare, the "Qimmiq," as it also known, was once used by the Inuit people for transportation. 21

Cane Corso
Originally this breed was found in southern Italy, where it was used for boar hunting, herding cattle, and bear fighting. 4

Cardigan Welsh Corgi
Of the two types of Welsh Corgi, the Pembroke and the Cardigan, this is the older breed. 11

Caucasian Shepherd Dog
A big sheepdog, the Caucasian Shepherd Dog is popular in Russia, Georgia, Armenia, and Azerbaijan. 20

Cavachon
A cross between a Cavalier King Charles Spaniel and Bichon Frise. 22

Cavalier King Charles Spaniel
This is one of the largest of the toy breeds. It was named for the English king, Charles II. 16, 24

Cesky Fousek
A Czech breed, this gundog is equally at home on land or in water. 18

Cesky Terrier
Bred in Eastern Europe in the 1940s, this was a cross between a Sealyham Terrier and a Scottish Terrier. 14

Chesapeake Bay Retriever
Named for Chesapeake Bay in Virginia, America, these dogs love water. Their thick coats keep them warm and dry. 8

Chihuahua
From Chihuahua in Mexico, this is the world's smallest breed. It was first known as the Arizona Dog or Texas Dog. 17, 24

Chinese Crested
Thought to have come from Africa, not China, Chinese Cresteds were traded at sea ports so are now found around the world. 17

Chinese Shar-pei
One of the oldest known dog breeds, the Chinese Shar-pei has distinctive loose folds of skin and a blue-black tongue. 13

Chinook
Chinooks were originally bred in North America to pull sleds. They were used on the first expedition to Antarctica in 1929. 5

Chorkie
A cross between a Chihuahua and a Yorkshire Terrier. 22

Chow Chow
Originally a Chinese hunting dog, the Chow Chow was bred two thousand years ago or more. It is one of only two breeds with a black tongue, the other being the Chinese Shar-pei. 12

Doberman Pinscher

Chow Pei
A cross between a Chow Chow and a Chinese Shar-pei. 22

Chowman Shepherd
A cross between a Chow Chow and a German Shepherd Dog. 23

Cirneco dell'Etna
Originally from the island of Sicily in Italy, this small hound was used to hunt rabbits. 7

Clumber Spaniel
Once popular with the British royal family, this is the largest of all Spaniel breeds. 8

Cockapoo
A cross between a Cocker Spaniel and a Poodle. 22

Cocker Spaniel
This very old breed used to hunt woodcock. They have a powerful sense of smell. 9

Collie
This very energetic breed is traditionally used for herding sheep. 11

Coton de Tulear
A small, soft, fluffy dog, it is named for its cotton-like coat and the city of Tuléar in Madagascar where it was first bred. 13

Curly-coated Retriever
This waterfowl hunter is one of the oldest, and the tallest, of the Retriever breeds. 8

Dachshund
A German breed, the Dachshund was first used to hunt badgers. Unusually, it can hunt both above and below ground. 6, 24

Dalmatian
When Dalmatians are born they are pure white. Only after a few weeks do their spots begin to appear. 12

Dandie Dinmont Terrier
This rare Terrier comes from the border areas between Scotland and England, and was used to hunt otters, rabbits, and rats. 14

Doberman Pinscher
The Doberman Pinscher was bred by a German tax collector, Louis Doberman, who wanted a dog to protect him when he was visiting dangerous places. 5

Dobernauzer
A cross between a Doberman Pinscher and a Giant Schnauzer. 22

Dogo Argentino
This muscular white dog is a mastiff. It was bred to hunt larger animals, such as boar. 21

Dogue de Bordeaux
This stocky dog is a very ancient French breed. It was trained to hunt, fight, protect, and herd. 5

Dorgi
A cross between a Dachshund and a Pembroke Welsh Corgi. 23

Dog Breeds

Drever
Introduced to Sweden from Germany, this hound was once used to track deer. 18

Dutch Partridge Dog
Also known as a Drent, this is a favorite gundog in the Netherlands where it was bred. 18

English Cocker Spaniel
The English Cocker Spaniel can be many different colors, including black, golden, orange and white, and red. 8, 25

English Foxhound
The English Foxhound was bred in the 16th century by mixing the Greyhound with the Fox Terrier and the Bulldog. 6

English Setter
This gundog has a speckled pattern to its coat that is known as "belton." 8, 25

English Springer Spaniel
This small hunting dog is called Springer because it was trained to "spring," or flush, birds into the air. 8, 24

English Toy Spaniel
The Toy Spaniel was once used to hunt birds, but later became a favorite with the English royal family as a companion dog. 17

Entlebucher Mountain Dog
This is the smallest of the four Swiss mountain hound breeds. All four Mountain Dogs have a distinctive three-color coat: black with patches of light-brown and white on their faces, chests, and legs. 11

Estrela Mountain Dog
From the mountains of Estrela in Portugal, the Estrela is an exceptionally good guard dog. 18

Field Spaniel
The glossy-coated Field Spaniel is an increasingly rare breed in the UK. 7

Finnish Lapphund
Finnish people, the Sami, used this breed to herd reindeer in the Arctic. 11

Finnish Spitz
The "Finkie" is the national dog of Finland. This breed is a "bark pointer," which means it barks when it finds its prey. 13

Flat-coated Retriever
This highly versatile gundog was extremely popular both in both America and Britain in the 19th century. It was a favorite of gamekeepers. 8

French Bulldog
A descendant of the English Bulldog, the French Bulldog has bat-shaped ears. 13, 24

French Spaniel
The French Spaniel is taller than the English Springer Spaniel. 19

Gerberian Shepsky
A cross between a German Shepherd Dog and a Siberian Husky. 23

German Pinscher
This is a German working dog. It can come in many different colors, including black, blue, red, and brown. 4

German Shepherd Dog
Also known as the Alsatian, this dog is famous for its agility and intelligence. 11

German Shorthaired Pointer
This German gundog's short, thick hair helps it to stay warm and dry in water. 9

German Spitz
This Spitz has a distinctive fox-like face and a bushy tail that curves over its back. 18, 25

German Wirehaired Pointer
This eager hunting dog has a very thick wiry coat that protects it from thorny bushes and wet weather. 8

Giant Schnauzer
The Giant Schnauzer was originally used as a sheepdog in Germany. It has thick eyebrows and a beard. 4

Glen of Imaal Terrier
A short-legged Terrier from Ireland, the Glen of Imaal Terrier is also known at the Wicklow Terrier, or simply Glen. 15

Golden Retriever
One of the world's most popular breeds, the dog originates from Scotland where it was bred to work over long distances and rocky ground to retrieve birds. 8

Goldendoodle
A cross between a Golden Retriever and a Poodle. 22

Gollie
A cross between a Golden Retriever and a Collie. 23

Gordon Setter
Named for a Scottish aristocrat, the Duke of Gordon, this hunting dog is distinctive for its black-and-tan coloring. 8

Grand Basset Griffon Vendéen
A pack hound, the Grand Bassett was bred to catch hares. 19

Grand Bleu de Gascogne
An old French hunting breed, it gets its name from the blue color of its coat. 19

Great Dane
The world record for the tallest dog is held by a Great Dane. Surprisingly, the Great Dane comes from Germany, not Denmark. 5, 25

Great Pyrenees
This ancient breed of big, white sheepdog originates from the Pyrenees mountains in southern France and northern Spain. 5

Greater Swiss Mountain Dog
The Greater Swiss Mountain Dog is an especially good watchdog. 4

Greenland Dog
This husky-type dog comes from Greenland, where it was used to pull sleds and hunt seals. 20

Greyhound
The Greyhound can reach a speed of up to 43 miles per hour. 6

Hamilton Hound
This Swedish hunting hound has a white stripe on its head, four white paws, and a white tip on its tail. 18

Harrier
The Harrier is smaller than the English Foxhound and bigger than the Beagle. It is a very popular hunting dog in Ireland. 6

Havanese
The Havanese is the national dog of Cuba. It may have arrived in Cuba from the island of Tenerife in the 16th century. 17

Horgi
A cross between a Siberian Husky and one of the Welsh Corgis. 23

Hovawart
A very old German breed, this working dog comes in three colors: black, black and gold, and blond. 18

Huskamute
A cross between a Siberian Husky and an Alaskan Malamute. 23

Ibizan Hound
Originally from the Middle East, this hound survived on the Spanish Balearic Islands where it was used to hunt rabbits. 7

Icelandic Sheepdog
In the 17th century, Icelandic Sheepdogs were imported into England where they became popular. One is even mentioned in Shakespeare's play *Henry V*. 11

Irish Red and White Setter
Believed to be the older of the two Irish setters, Red and White Setters may have been bred in the 18th century. 8

Irish Setter
The Irish Setter is known for its glossy red coat. 9

Irish Terrier
The Irish Terrier was used by the British Army in both World War I and World War II. 14

Irish Water Spaniel
This Irish breed is believed to be more than a thousand years old. 9

Irish Wolfhound
A very ancient breed, the Irish Wolfhound is the largest and tallest of all the hound breeds. 7

Italian Greyhound
This greyhound was popular with British royalty, including King James I and Queen Victoria. 17

Italian Pointer
A gun dog, the "Bracco" has a long ears and a drooping mouth that seem to give it a sad face. 19

Jack Russell Cattle Dog
A cross between a Jack Russell Terrier and an Australian Cattle Dog. 22

Jack Russell Terrier
This Terrier is named for the Reverend John Russell, a 19th-century English dog breeder. 18

Jagdterrier
Known as the German Hunt Terrier, this small dog is a fearless hunter. 18

Japanese Chin
A pair of these Japanese dogs was given to Queen Victoria by an American naval officer, Commodore Perry, in 1853. 16

Jindo
This hunting dog comes from Korea, where it is considered a national treasure. 21

Jug
A cross between a Jack Russell Terrier and a Pug. 22

Kai Ken
The Kai Ken is very rare and is considered the oldest and most pure breed in Japan. 21

Karelian Bear Dog
From Finland, this brave little hunting dog was once used to hunt bears. 19

Keeshond
Sometimes called the Dutch barge dog, this breed comes from The Netherlands where it was used to guard boats. 13

Kerry Blue Terrier
When they are puppies, Kerry Blue Terriers are black. As they grow up, their coats turn blue. 14

Kishu Ken
Kishu Kens are strong athletic hunting dogs from Japan. They were originally bred to hunt boar and deer in the mountains. 20

Komondor
The Komondor looks like a huge mop. It was originally used in Hungary to guard farm animals. 5

Kooikerhondje
This Dutch dog is a "tolling" breed, which means it was used to lure birds out into the open for the hunter. 18

Kuvasz
A very large, white dog, the Kuvasz was once a favorite with the kings of Hungary, who used them as guard dogs. 5

Labradoodle
A cross between a Labrador Retriever and a Poodle. 23

Labrador Retriever
The Labrador originates from Newfoundland in Canada. 9

Lagotto Romagnolo
An ancient breed of Italian hunting dog, the Lagotto is now used for hunting truffles. 9

Lakeland Terrier
The Lakeland Terrier comes from the Lake District in England. Foxes were hunted on foot in this mountainous area and the dogs were known for their stamina. 15

Lancashire Heeler
This small herding dog may have been bred from a Welsh Corgi and a Manchester Terrier. 18

Large Münsterländer
Originally from Münster in Germany, the Large Münsterländer is a natural pointer. 19

Leonberger
During World War II these giant working dogs from Germany were used to pull ammunition carts. 4

Lhasa Apso
The Lhasa Apso comes from Tibet. Its long coat and facial hair help to protect it from the wind and cold. 12

Longdog
A cross between a Greyhound and a Deerhound. 22

Löwchen
Also known as the Little Lion Dog, this is one of the world's rarest breeds. 13

Maltese
This very old breed, thought to be from Malta, may have been brought back to Europe by the Crusaders. 17

Manchester Terrier
These rat-catching Terriers were popular in farming and mining areas in Northern England. 14

Mastiff
The Mastiff has been bred in England for over two thousand years. The breed fought alongside Britons against the invading Romans in 55 BCE. 4

Miniature American Shepherd
This new American breed is a very useful working dog. 10

Miniature Bull Terrier
In the 19th century, Bull Terriers were the size of Miniature Bull Terriers. 15

Miniature Pinscher
The much larger Doberman Pinscher was bred to look like the Miniature Pinscher. 16

Miniature Schnauzer
A German breed known for its bearded snout, its name comes from the German word for snout, which can also mean moustache. 15, 25

Mountain Cur
Curs were brought to America from Europe. Today the Mountain Cur is used mostly for hunting in the Southern United States. 21

Mudi
Like the Pumi and the Puli, this herding dog comes from Hungary. 19

Neapolitan Mastiff
This huge Italian dog was used as a guard dog even in Ancient Roman times. 5

Newfoundland
A great swimmer, this big dog has a heavy coat to keep it warm in freezing waters. 4

Norfolk Terrier
One of the smallest Terriers, the Norfolk has a wire-haired coat. It is very similar to the Norwich Terrier. 15

Norrbottenspets
Although this Swedish breed was first used as a hunting dog, it makes a good family pet. 19

Norwegian Buhund
"Bu" means farm in Norwegian. This little dog was used for herding in Scandinavia. 11

Norwegian Elkhound
The Vikings used Elkhounds as guard dogs, for hunting, and for herding animals. 7

Norwegian Lundehund
The Lundehund has six toes, which helps it to climb rock cliffs. It was originally used to hunt puffins in the Arctic Circle. 13

Norwich Terrier
The Norfolk Terrier has drop ears, while the Norwich Terrier has prick ears. 14

Nova Scotia Duck Tolling Retriever
The breed looks like a fox, but has white markings. It is used to "toll," or lure, curious birds toward hunters. 9

Old English Sheepdog
These lovable dogs have starred on TV and in many movies, including *Sesame Street*, *Chitty Chitty Bang Bang*, and *101 Dalmatians*. 11, 25

Otterhound
A rare hound breed, this shaggy dog swims well and was used to hunt otters. 6

Papillon
This dog has butterfly-shaped ears, which can be either upright or drooping. Papillon means butterfly. 16

Parson Russell Terrier
With a narrow, flexible chest, this strong Terrier was bred to dig foxes out of holes. 14

Peekapoo
A cross between a Pekingese and a Poodle. 23

Pekingese
Also known as Lion Dog, Sun Dog, or Sleeve Dog, Pekingese were kept by the Imperial family in China, and considered sacred. 17

Pembroke Welsh Corgi
Queen Elizabeth II of England was given a Pembroke Welsh Corgi called Susan on her 18th birthday. All the Queen's Corgis are descended from this dog. 11

Peruvian Hairless Dog
It is believed that the ancient Inca people kept hairless dogs, so this breed may be a descendant of those animals. 21

Löwchen

Dog Breeds

Petit Basset Griffon Vendéen
Known as Griffs and Petits, these small, short-legged French hounds are good at picking up scent and hunting in rough terrain. 7

Pharaoh Hound
The national dog of Malta, this hound was used for hunting rabbits. 7

Plott
One of the six Coonhound breeds, the Plott was bred in North Carolina and named for two German boys, Enoch and Johannes Plott, who emigrated to America in 1750. 6

Pointer
This is one of the oldest breeds of hunting dog. When it points, by standing motionless looking at prey, it will often also lift one of its legs. 9

Polish Lowland Sheepdog
The "PON" (Polski Owczarek Nizinny in Polish) is a shaggy-coated sheep dog. 11

Pomeranian
Queen Victoria had a much-loved Pomeranian called Marco. These sturdy little dogs make loyal companions. 16, 24

Poodle
Winston Churchill, a British Prime Minister in the 1940s and 1950s, had two Poodles, one called Rufus I and one called Rufus II. 12, 25

Portuguese Podengo Pequeno
This is the small version of an ancient hunting dog from Portugal. 6

Portuguese Pointer
The British may have brought this Portuguese dog to England in the 18th century, and bred from it the English Pointer. 19

Portuguese Water Dog
US President Barack Obama chose this breed as a pet for his two daughters. 5

Pug
The perfect pug tail should have two tight curls. The breed originated in China but became very popular with royalty in Europe. 16, 25

Puggle
A cross between a Pug and a Beagle. 23

Puli
This small sheepdog, which is originally from Hungary, has a corded coat. The breed is usually black. 11

Pumi
A herding dog, the Pumi comes from Hungary, but is now most popular in Finland. 19

Pyrenean Mastiff
These dogs used to guard flocks of sheep in the Kingdom of Aragon in Spain. 19

Pyrenean Shepherd
Like the Great Pyrenees breed, this herding dog comes from Pyrenees mountains in northern Spain and southern France. 10

Rat Terrier
An American breed, the Rat Terrier was bred from Fox Terriers and other Terriers that had been brought to the United States by early immigrants. 14

Redbone Coonhound
The Redbone Coonhound is a very useful hunter and has a distinctive red coat. 7

Rhodesian Ridgeback
Also known at the Lion Dog, this powerful African dog has a ridge of hairs running down its back that point in the opposite direction to the rest of its hair. 7

Rottweiler
The Rottweiler is a powerful dog — it once used to herd, drive livestock, and pull carts. 5, 24

Russell Terrier
This breed, popular in America, came from England and was developed in Australia. 15

Russian Toy
One of the smallest dogs in the world, this breed was once popular with the Russian aristocracy. 21

Saluki
Salukis come from the Middle East and originally hunted in packs to catch foxes, hares, and even gazelles. 7

Samoyed
These fluffy white dogs were originally used to herd animals and pull sleds in Siberia. 4

Schipperke
This small, fluffy black dog was originally used as a watchdog and for catching rats. 12

Schnoodle
A cross between a Schnauzer and a Poodle. 23

Scottish Deerhound
Larger than a Greyhound, the Scottish Deerhound has a tail so long that it almost touches the ground. 6

Scottish Terrier
Known as the Scottie, this breed was kept by gamekeepers in Scotland to help catch rats and other vermin. 15

Sealyham Terrier
This Welsh Terrier was bred at Sealyham House in Pembrokeshire, England, by Captain John Edwardes. Its white coat made it stand out from its quarry. 14

Shetland Sheepdog
Known as the Sheltie, this is one of the world's cleverest dog breeds. 11

Shiba Inu
One of the most popular dogs in Japan, this sturdy little breed is a great hunter. 12

Shih Tzu
In Tibet, these dogs were used by monks to raise the alarm. Shih Tzu means Lion Dog in Chinese. 17, 24

Shikoku
This breed is also known as the Japanese Wolf Dog. 20

Shorthaired Italian Hound
One of the most popular breeds in Italy, this hound is now kept mainly as a hunting dog. 18

Siberian Husky
Siberian Huskies can have either blue or brown eyes. They howl rather than bark. 4

Silky Terrier
This Australian breed is a mixture of the Australian Terrier and the Yorkshire Terrier. 16

Skye Terrier
Noted for its long coat, this rare Terrier was originally used to hunt otter and fox on the Isle of Skye in Scotland. 15

Sloughi
The Sloughi originates from North Africa where it was used for hunting. 6

Slovakian Hound
This small black hound was bred to hunt boar in Eastern Europe. 19

Smooth Fox Terrier
Smooth Fox Terriers with white coats were the most valuable kind because they were less likely to be confused with foxes during a hunt. 15

Soft Coated Wheaten Terrier
This is one of four Terrier breeds that come from Ireland. 15

Spanish Water Dog
The Spanish Water Dog is related to the Portuguese Water Dog. 11

Spinone Italiano
A large hunting dog from Piedmont in Italy, the Spinone is one of the oldest breeds. 8

Sprocker
A cross between an English Springer Spaniel and a Cocker Spaniel. 22

St. Bernard
The St. Bernard is famous for helping to find people who are trapped under snow in the Alp mountains. It is the heaviest breed of dog. 5, 25

Stabyhoun
A national treasure in the Netherlands, the Stabyhoun is one of the world's rarest breeds. 18

Staffordshire Bull Terrier
The Staffie was once used for bull- and bear-baiting. 15, 24

Standard Schnauzer
This working dog was used in Europe throughout the Middle Ages. 4

Sussex Spaniel
The Sussex Spaniel is thought to be the best watchdog of all Spaniels. 9

Pug

Polish Lowland Sheepdog

Silky Terrier

Swedish Vallhund
This short-legged herding dog may have been used by the Vikings for herding cattle. 11

Thai Ridgeback
There are only three Ridgeback purebreds. This one comes from Thailand. 20

Tibetan Mastiff
The Tibetan Mastiff was trained to protect sheep from wild animals such as wolves, tigers, and bears. 4

Tibetan Spaniel
Perhaps the ancestor of the Cavalier King Charles Spaniel, this breed may be more than two-and-a-half thousand years old. 12

Tibetan Terrier
Tibetan Terriers have large, flat feet that help them to walk on snow, and long eyelashes that shield their eyes from falling snow. 12

Toy Fox Terrier
An American breed, the Toy Fox Terrier is calmer and smaller than the Fox Terrier. 17

Toy Manchester Terrier
This is a miniature version of the standard Manchester Terrier. 16

Toy Poodle
Known for its intelligence, the Poodle comes from Germany, although it is considered the national dog of France. The Toy Poodle is smaller than the standard Poodle. 16

Transylvanian Hound
This big black-and-tan hunting dog was once popular with the nobility of Transylvania. 19

Treeing Tennessee Brindle
These brindle-colored cur dogs are trained to chase animals up trees. 21

Treeing Walker Coonhound
Descended from the American and English Foxhounds, this American hound is strong and active and can climb trees. 6

Vizsla
Originally a hunting dog from Hungary, the Vizsla is now a popular family dog. 8

Weimaraner
This highly energetic German hunting dog has blue-gray eyes. 9

Welsh Springer Spaniel
This red and white sporting dog was very popular in 1700s among English nobility. 9

Welsh Terrier
Former US President J.F. Kennedy had a pet Welsh Terrier called Charlie. 15

West Highland White Terrier
The distinctive white Westie originally came from Scotland, where it was used on large estates to hunt game and vermin. 15, 24

Welsh Terrier

Westiepoo
A cross between a West Highland White Terrier and a Poodle. 22

Whippet
These small hounds were very popular with factory workers and miners in Northern England in the 19th century. 7

Wire Fox Terrier
This long-legged Terrier is renowned for its stamina, courage, and gentle nature. 14

Wirehaired Pointing Griffon
This energetic dog has an especially good sense of smell. 9

Wirehaired Vizsla
Heavier and sturdier than the Vizsla, the Wirehaired Vizsla has a rough coat that helps it to cope with wet weather. 9

Xoloitzcuintli
An ancient hairless dog from Mexico, the "Xolo" is adapted to living in tropical climates. 13

Yorkipoo
A cross between a Yorkshire Terrier and a Poodle. 22

Yorkshire Terrier
Weavers in Northern England used to keep these dogs to catch rats in cloth factories. 17

A Firefly Book

Published by Firefly Books Ltd. 2018
Copyright © 2018 Eight Books Ltd.
Text copyright © 2018 Mark Fletcher
Illustrations copyright © 2018 Jim Medway

First Printing

Library of Congress Control Number: 2018934003

Library and Archives Canada Cataloguing in Publication
Medway, Jim, author
    Big dogs, little dogs : a visual guide to the world's dogs / Jim Medway.
Includes index.
Previously published: 2016.
ISBN 978-0-228-10108-6 (hardcover)
    1. Dog breeds--Pictorial works--Juvenile literature. 2. Dogs--Pictorial
works--Juvenile literature. 3. Dog breeds--Juvenile literature. 4. Dogs--
Juvenile literature. I. Title.
SF426.5.M44 2018   j636.7'1   C2018-900994-2

Published in Canada by
Firefly Books Ltd.
50 Staples Avenue, Unit 1
Richmond Hill, Ontario L4B 0A7

Published in the United States by
Firefly Books (U.S.) Inc.
P.O. Box 1338, Ellicott Station
Buffalo, New York, USA 14205

Printed in China

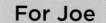

For Joe